# Choosing a Career in Animal Care

Animal care careers include working to protect wild birds and animals.

W♠W

# Choosing a Career in Animal Care

Jane Hurwitz

The Rosen Publishing Group, Inc.
New York

Published in 1997, 2001 by The Rosen Publishing Group, Inc.
29 East 21st Street, New York, NY 10010

Revised Edition 2001

Library of Congress Cataloging-in-Publication Data

Hurwitz, Jane.
  Choosing a career in animal care / Jane Hurwitz.—rev. ed.
    p.   cm.—(The world of work)
  Includes bibliographical references and index.
  Summary: Introduces careers as dog groomer, pet store clerk,
veterinarian, zoo keeper, and other animal-related careers.
    ISBN 0-8239-3356-3
    1. Animal Specialists—Vocational guidance—Juvenile literature. 2.
Animal specialists—Biography—Juvenile literature. [1. Animal
specialists—Vocational guidance. 2. Vocational guidance.
3. Occupations.] I. Title. II. Series: World of work (New York, NY)
SF80.H87  1996
636.08'3'023—dc20                                    96-9453
                                                         CIP
                                                         AC

*Manufactured in the United States of America*

# Contents

# Introduction

*G*rowing up, Susan lived in the country, and while her family didn't have a farm or anything like that, they did have a lot of pets. Susan spent most of her time hiking in the forests near the house. Her best friend had a horse and taught Susan how to ride.

Even though she studied Animal Science in college, when Susan's friend asked her to share an apartment in the city, she couldn't resist. But Susan did worry that she'd end up being a waitress or a salesperson and waste her college education. Luckily, her friend's boyfriend worked for the city's Department of Parks & Recreation. When he found out Susan had a degree in Animal Science and knew how to ride a horse, he suggested she become a park ranger.

Now Susan's learning about the wildlife that thrives here in the city. Soon she'll be educating visitors about the

Many people in animal care have loved animals since they were kids.

*animals that live here and guiding tourists around the park. To Susan, this is the best of both worlds!*

There are many different careers within the world of animal care. The one thing they all have in common is that they focus on the care and protection of animals. These careers fall into two categories: working directly or indirectly with animals. People who work directly with animals, caring for their health and well-being, include veterinarians, pet groomers, and zookeepers. People who work indirectly with animals, protecting their rights and supplying pet-care products, include animal rights activists and those who work in pet supply stores.

People choose animal care careers for many reasons. Most people just love animals. Many of these people are happiest when they work directly with animals. Satisfying jobs for this kind of person might be animal groomer, large animal veterinarian (a vet who works with farm and other large animals), or seeing-eye dog trainer. Other people find personal satisfaction in helping animals in distress. Ideal jobs for such a person might include animal shelter worker, veterinarian, and animal rights activist.

And then there are the pets. People who live in the United States have more than 62 million dogs and 64 million cats as pets. They own about 28 million birds, and 13 million exotic pets. The pet-care industry offers jobs for those who want to help keep pets happy and healthy.

# Questions to Ask Yourself

If any of these areas sound interesting to you, a career in animal care may be the right choice for you. There are many careers in which people can work with animals. Would you prefer to work directly or indirectly with animals? Why? What sort of animals would you like to work with?

Love and respect for animals is the first requirement for a career in animal care.

# Career Possibilities in Animal Care

B ecoming aware of your attitudes and personality traits can help you decide whether a career in animal care is right for you.

## Are You an Animal Lover?

Do you care about the fair treatment of animals? This is probably the most important personality trait to have if you want to work with animals. It's also a good indication that you're an animal lover.

Besides loving animals, you must have a professional attitude that will allow you to function in difficult situations. Veterinary assistants often work with animals that have been abused. Animal shelter workers sometimes need to destroy, or kill, unwanted or unhealthy animals. This is called euthanasia. Animal care workers must accept these difficult aspects of caring for animals.

While many people are animal lovers, not all animal lovers will find animal care careers satisfying. Working with animals is rarely glamorous

**11**

and is often demanding. Cages need to be cleaned. Animals sometimes live in temperatures that are uncomfortable for humans. Taking care of animals' needs often requires long hours of hard work.

The majority of animal care workers earn modest incomes. Many careers in animal care require experience that is gained through low-paying entry-level jobs. Some careers even start out as volunteer work with no pay at all. Other careers require college courses or advanced college degrees. When considering an animal care career, you must decide what type of training you are willing to go through. You must also learn whether it is available and affordable for you.

## Do You Have What It Takes?

There are so many jobs in the field of animal care that it may be hard to know where to start. The first step is to think about your skills and interests. What do you like to do? What don't you like to do? Think about the type of environment you prefer to be in and whether you like to study. These things play a part in helping you decide what career path you want to follow. Look at the following questions. Your answers can help you decide whether you should explore an animal care career.

✔ Do you like animals?

✔ Are you willing to be responsible for the health and well-being of animals?

✔ Have you ever done any volunteer work with animals?

✔ Do you prefer to work indoors or outdoors?

✔ Are you willing to get training or further education to work well with animals?

✔ Are you outgoing?

✔ Do you like to be around other people?

✔ Do you prefer to work alone?

✔ Do you plan ahead?

✔ Do you manage your time well?

✔ Do you have a good rapport with animals?

✔ Do you feel comfortable with all animals or only with certain kinds?

✔ Are you looking to earn a large income?

Your answers can help you identify some of your strengths and preferences and help you decide whether or not you should work in the field of animal care. They can also help you decide what career within the field of animal care interests you the most. For instance, if you like to work outdoors, you may enjoy being a zookeeper or a large animal veterinarian. If you like to work alone, you may not want to work in a pet supply store where you will have to deal with coworkers and the public. Keep your answers in mind as you read about the different careers that are available.

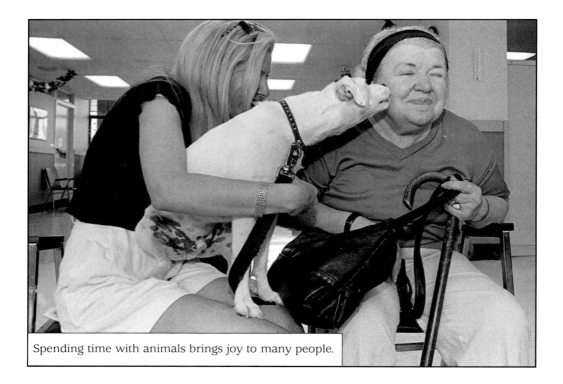

Spending time with animals brings joy to many people.

Johnson volunteered with a group called Pets for Life. The group met once a month after school. Pets for Life took cats and dogs to visit elderly residents of nursing homes. Johnson enjoyed working with people and thought that volunteering was a good way to make new friends. He also liked working with animals.

The nursing home residents really enjoyed the visits. The animals also served as therapy. They added excitement to the residents' day. The nursing home patients, who often felt lonely, cheered up at the sight of a friendly dog or cuddly cat.

Johnson soon realized that his respect for animals had grown. He had always liked animals, but his visits with

*Pets for Life had shown him what an impact animals can have on humans. Johnson also became concerned about the impact that people have on animals.*

*Johnson knew that he wanted a career that involved being around animals as well as people. He thought about careers in animal care. He knew about veterinarians since he had taken his dog to the vet many times. He also knew that the animals at the zoo had caretakers. Volunteering gave Johnson new ideas about his future career path. How could he narrow down the choices to one career? What would satisfy his interest in helping both people and animals?*

*Johnson's next step was to evaluate his skills and interests. He identified his strengths and weaknesses. Then he decided that he wanted to own a pet store. He began by getting an after-school job at the local pet-supply store.*

## Questions to Ask Yourself

There are certain attitudes or traits that a person must have to be successful and happy in a career in animal care. 1) Are you an animal lover? 2) Do you care so much for them that providing care for them every day would make you happy?

# Noncollege Careers in Animal Care

The best known medical career for animal lovers is that of veterinarian. But it is not the only choice. There are a variety of other medical careers from which to choose.

*Steve works as a veterinary technician at a horse hospital. He loves it because he never has the same workday twice.*

*Steve starts at 7:00 AM with rounds at the stables. He checks on horses that are recuperating from illness or surgery. If an animal has problems, Steve makes a note for the head veterinarian.*

*Steve also talks to the people who work in the barn. They clean the stalls and feed the horses. They also exercise horses that are able to leave their stalls. Since they spend most of their time around horses, they often know best how an animal is doing.*

*At 8:00 AM Steve reviews his duty list for the day. This list is prepared by the hospital office manager. Without a duty list, Steve couldn't coordinate his duties with the needs of the veterinarians. His list tells him what surgeries are scheduled and when. Steve also needs to know the number of examinations scheduled.*

*By 8:30 AM Steve starts to prepare for the day's surgeries. Most surgeries are scheduled during the morning. Steve makes sure that the two operating rooms are stocked with all the necessary supplies. Then he prepares the horses for surgery. Sometimes this means taking blood samples or shaving the area to be operated on. After each surgery, Steve writes up the surgery notes. He also files X rays and processes laboratory samples.*

*After lunch, Steve's work is mostly clerical. He orders supplies and medicine. He takes the temperature and vital signs of horses scheduled for appointments.*

*Every afternoon, Steve organizes and sterilizes all the operating equipment. If there is an emergency, the veterinarians may need to operate immediately, sometimes even in the middle of the night.*

*At 3:00 PM Steve visits the barn again. He checks on the animals that had surgery that morning. Steve looks in on the other horses. If any of them need attention, he calls the veterinarian scheduled for night duty.*

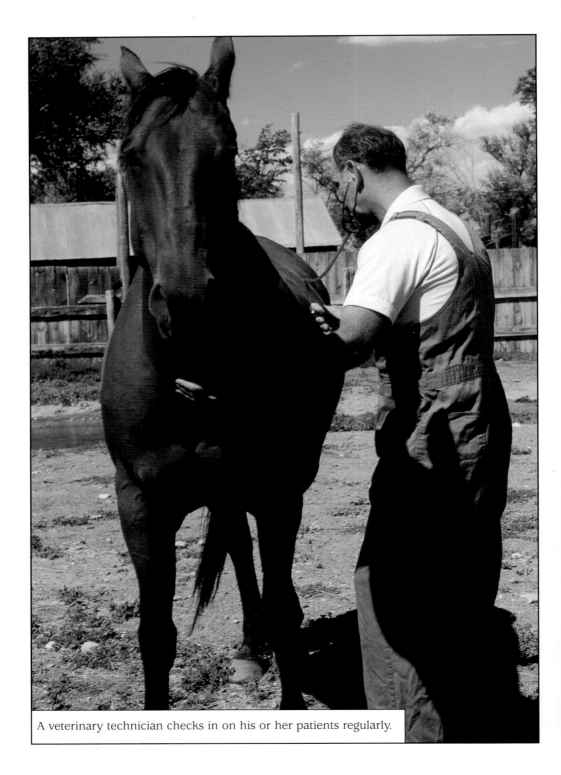

A veterinary technician checks in on his or her patients regularly.

*Steve usually finishes his barn visits by 4:00 PM, when he signs out at the main building. Steve enjoys his job. Each day something happens to let Steve know that he made the right choice in becoming a veterinary technician.*

Veterinary technicians do many things that veterinarians do. Their job duties include checking animals for disease, administering medicine, and taking X rays. Other duties include preparing animals for surgery and performing laboratory work. Technicians may also perform clerical work.

The work that veterinary technicians do can be compared to the duties of a registered nurse. Like nurses, they are professionals. Also like nurses, there are some medical duties that they may not perform. They cannot make diagnoses, perform surgery, or write prescriptions. Each state has specific laws covering these restrictions.

Wages for beginning veterinary technicians range from $12,000 to $19,000 a year. Experience and education, geographic location, and size of establishment all affect their salaries. Technicians with greater experience and education often earn from $17,000 to $28,000 a year.

Other benefits available to veterinary technicians are health insurance and paid vacations. Retirement programs also may be available. Benefits for technicians vary with each job.

Technicians may be promoted to jobs with more responsibilities. Promotions depend on continued education through professional seminars, the technician's attitude, and on-the-job performance.

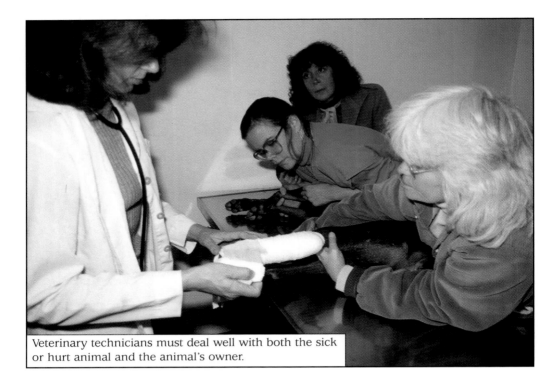
Veterinary technicians must deal well with both the sick or hurt animal and the animal's owner.

People who are interested in becoming veterinary technicians must enjoy working directly with animals. It also helps to be interested in science. Technicians must be able to work with other people as a team, since they may interact with other technicians and with animals' owners. They are always under the supervision of a veterinarian, senior technician, or scientist.

To become a veterinary technician you must complete a two-year training program. To enter training, you need a high school diploma. Studying chemistry, algebra, and biology in high school will be helpful. Training programs are offered at community colleges and technical schools. Programs usually include working in an animal hospital or veterinary office.

After completing a training program, many states require veterinary technicians to be registered.

Other states require certification. The American Veterinary Medical Association can provide information about these processes.

Part-time or volunteer work in an animal hospital or shelter can give you an idea whether you are suited to a veterinary technician career. Interviewing a variety of veterinary technicians also helps. Ask them where they trained and what experience they had before training. Find out what their current duties include. Choose technicians who work in different settings. Consider those who work in animal hospitals, animal shelters, or zoos. Research universities, pharmaceutical companies, and breeding kennels also hire veterinary technicians.

There are many advantages to a career as a veterinary technician. Technicians have a wide choice of work places. The job often provides good wages and benefits. It is a professional career with opportunity for growth and advancement.

But the career also has disadvantages. It is a medical job that involves seeing animals suffer and sometimes die. If watching a surgical operation bothers you, then this is probably not the job for you.

## Animal Care Attendant

Animal care attendants provide basic care for animals. Their duties may include feeding animals, cleaning cages, and ordering supplies. Attendants work in animal hospitals, animal shelters, stables, and laboratories. Animal care attendants do not need a high level of training. Most receive their training on the

Animal care attendants keep animals clean, fed, and comfortable.

job. As a result, animal care attendants are not highly paid. But this job provides experience for a person considering a career as a veterinary technician.

## Pet-Related Careers

Perhaps you are interested in working in a pet-related career. You could work with pets and their owners. Owning a pet shop is one example of a pet-related career. There are many types of pet-related businesses. Some require you to work indoors and have regular hours. These include working as a clerk, managing, or owning a pet store or kennel. Workers in other businesses, such as animal groomers and pet sitters, have more flexible hours. Jobs such as pet-walking and dog breeding require working outdoors.

*Growing up, all of the dogs José's family owned came from shelters, so they were usually mutts. He and his friends used to make fun of all those "fancy" dogs that had weird haircuts.*

*When José was sixteen he wanted to go on his class trip to Mexico. José's parents said okay but that he had to earn the money himself. José was having a hard time finding a decent job when his aunt suggested that he work for her at the animal salon. José was desperate, so he said okay.*

*José started out just answering the phones and washing the dogs occasionally. It didn't take long, however, before he was beginning to really enjoy it. It was fun to work with the animals and José began to see all the stuff he had thought of as crazy as creative instead. José began to almost feel like an artist.*

*José kept working there after his trip to Mexico, and now he's a grooming assistant. Who knows? Maybe José will open his own shop one day.*

Pet groomers work with both dogs and cats, although they are usually associated more with dogs. Being a pet groomer isn't just about washing and styling but involves some physical work as well. Keep in mind that some dogs can weigh over fifty pounds! You have to be able to carry and restrain an animal while you groom it.

You can become a pet groomer by either going to a special grooming school or by becoming an apprentice to a groomer. Being an apprentice means that you learn by working alongside an experienced professional. You might not get paid very much, but you learn everything you need to know by actually doing it. Groomers don't just work in pet salons. Many work in kennels or animal spas—places where pets go for a little pampering that includes not only grooming but special things like long walks and massages.

Being a pet groomer can be great if you enjoy working with animals. You don't have to go to college, you can often have flexible hours (some shops stay open late so that people can pick up their pets after work), and you can be creative. Transforming a dirty, scruffy dog into one that is sleek and well-groomed can be very satisfying.

Pet groomers are generally paid on commission, which means their income is based on the number of animals they groom. The average grooming takes about an hour and a half and costs around $45. The groomer usually gets to keep half while the rest goes to the salon or kennel.

To be a successful pet groomer you need to be able to work with both animals and people. You have to make both feel at ease and relaxed. Remember, many people think of their pets as children, so they might feel anxious leaving them with you. Also, keep in mind that dogs and cats can be very noisy, especially if they are frightened. If you can handle the noise and keep the animals calm and under control, this might be a good job for you.

If you love animals, you may enjoy working in a pet store.

## Pet Store Employee

If you'd like to share your love of animals and you like the challenge of matching a person to a pet, you might find working in a pet store very rewarding. Some of the responsibilities of this job include educating customers on the care and feeding of a pet, taking care of the pets themselves, and helping people decide on an animal to take home.

## Animal Trainers

If an animal needs to learn a behavior or a skill, owners will take them to an animal trainer. Trainers teach animals to obey, to be a guard or narcotics dog, or to work with other animals. Animal trainers work by using voice, hand signals, or contact commands. In addition to learning skills, some animals are trained to perform for competitions or animal shows.

## Laboratory Animal Caretakers

Some caretakers are interested in research that is done with animals. Laboratory animal caretakers work with scientists, doctors, veterinarians, and other laboratory technicians. Some of the things they do include feeding and taking care of the animals—which can include mice, sheep, rats, monkeys, and rabbits—as well as giving them medicines. Caretakers often have to keep detailed records of what treatment was given to an animal and what the reaction to it was. This is not a job for the faint of heart, as caretakers have to watch out for diseases, illnesses, and injuries to the animals.

## Kennel Worker

Kennels board and groom pets. Like pet groomers, kennel workers must know as much as possible about the different breeds of dogs and cats. They are responsible for the animals' total care—from feeding and exercise to cleaning and petting. Starting salaries range from $12,000 to $23,000 a year.

## Pet Therapist

A pet therapist is someone who feels they can communicate with an animal and uses this communication to help figure out behavior problems.

Many people believe that animals communicate by sending and receiving mental pictures. A pet owner might bring their pet to a pet therapist because of behavior problems like going to the bathroom on the carpet or constantly scratching a piece of furniture, or because they think their pet is depressed. A pet therapist will communicate with the animal to find out the cause of the behavior and help both the owner and animal to overcome the problem.

As this is a relatively new field, there are no professional standards for it nor are there many established schools. A therapist should have training in psychology and animal behavior as well as a strong concern for the well-being of animals. Many veterinary practices that advertise a holistic approach offer pet therapy.

## Pet Sitters and Dog Walkers

Pet sitters take care of animals while their owners are away. They come to the house, feed the pet, play with it and, if needed, make sure it gets proper exercise. They make sure that the pets are cared for while their owners are out of town.

Dog walkers will come to a person's home to take their dog out for a walk. They come anywhere from once to three times a day. Oftentimes, people will want their dogs walked once in the morning and once in the evening.

Both of these jobs require you to be trust-worthy because the owners will generally leave you their house keys. You must be responsible

Pet owners trust kennel workers to take good care of their pets.

enough to remember the animal's specific needs, particularly if they need any medication. You must also know what to do if there's an emergency and arrive at the times requested. These jobs generally pay per visit or walk. Rates range from $5 to over $25 a day, depending on the requirements. Only a few people manage to make this a full-time career, but many enjoy it as a part-time job.

## Protection and Conservation

There are many careers that involve protecting animals and their habitats. Park rangers, fish biologists, and range managers are a few. Some zoos also work to protect animals by breeding rare species in captivity.

*It isn't easy to get a job at a zoo. There aren't many zoos, so competition for jobs is tough. Many of the positions require advanced education. Other jobs are very specialized. Elaine had to plan carefully to get her job.*

*Elaine's plan was to volunteer to work at the zoo, which she did during her senior year of high school. That gave Elaine valuable experience. As a volunteer, she gained an edge over other applicants. Elaine wanted to have the best possible chance of getting a full-time position.*

*Elaine's first duty as a volunteer was cleaning the exhibits in the children's zoo. She also worked one shift a week in the zoo's nursery. Elaine bottle-fed baby animals. She also learned how to mix foods for animals that were on special diets. Elaine loved it. She decided that a permanent job in the zoo's nursery would be perfect for her. Elaine's volunteer work gave her great on-the-job experience. It also convinced her that a job working at a zoo would be a fulfilling career.*

*Something else Elaine learned was the great amount of work zoos do to educate the public. She saw that people learned from observing animals. More than ever, she wanted a job there. But there were no openings.*

Some zoos work to protect animals by keeping and breeding rare species.

*After high school Elaine found a job at a veterinarian's office. Her year of volunteer work at the zoo gave her the experience she needed to get that job. Elaine fed the animals that were boarded at the veterinarian's and made sure they had plenty of water. She also worked in the office answering the phones and greeting incoming patients and their owners.*

*Although Elaine was working full-time, she continued to volunteer at the zoo. That didn't leave her much spare time. But Elaine still hoped that a position at the zoo would open up. She wanted to be right there when one did.*

*Finally, at the end of her second year as a volunteer, the zoo had an opening. The large mammal exhibit needed an assistant zookeeper. The keeper would be responsible for feeding, cleaning, and exercising the African elephants. Other work in the large mammal exhibit building would also be assigned.*

*Thanks to her volunteer experience, Elaine was given an interview for the position. The supervisor knew she was a volunteer. Elaine's donated time showed the supervisor that Elaine was committed to working for the zoo, and she got the job!*

*Elaine's work is hard. It involves a lot of physical labor. She hauls hay and crates of vegetables for the elephants to eat. She also helps bathe the elephants with a high-power hose and a giant brush. Elaine often gets wet or muddy and stays that way for most of the day. But working around animals as amazing as elephants makes Elaine's career worthwhile.*

Most zookeepers take care of the animals' daily needs. They clean the exhibits and feed the animals, many of whom require special diets. Zookeepers also watch over the animals in their care. A change in animals' behavior may mean that something is wrong with them. A zookeeper must be a trained observer.

Salaries for zookeepers depend on the size of the zoo and on the keeper's experience. The range for beginning salaries is from $16,000 to $37,000 a year. More experienced zookeepers can earn $28,000 to $86,000 a year.

Zookeepers must be able to shoulder a great deal of responsibility. They are directly responsible for the health and safety of animals in their care. Good communication skills are important, both when dealing with colleagues and with those under the keeper's direct authority. The public sees the zookeeper as an authority on animals. Keepers must be able to answer questions on animals' habits and diets.

Zookeepers are required to have a high school diploma. Some zoos also prefer that they take some college courses in biology or zoology. If you do not have formal education in zoology or animal

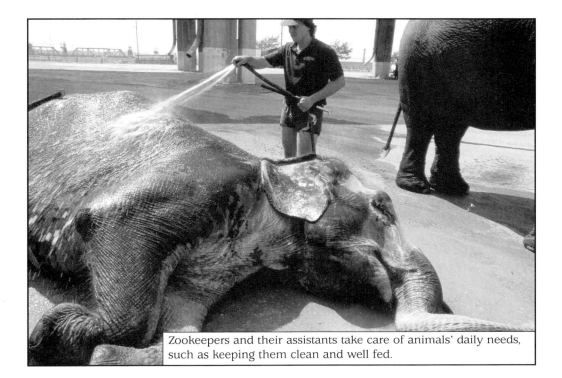

Zookeepers and their assistants take care of animals' daily needs, such as keeping them clean and well fed.

management, try volunteering at a zoo. This could give you the experience you need to secure an entry-level job as a zookeeper.

The advantages of working at a zoo can be enormous. There is a wide variety of unusual animals with which to work, many of them being endangered species. Helping maintain species that are threatened with extinction in the wild can be highly rewarding. There are some disadvantages, however. Much of a zookeeper's work is strenuous physical labor. Zoo animals need care every day of the year. This can lead to long work hours, often on holidays or weekends. New workers often work long shifts for low wages. But if it is work that you enjoy, the experience is critical and could lead to a lifelong, fulfilling career.

Zookeepers must watch the animals in their care for any changes in behavior.

## Wildlife Careers

There are opportunities to work with animals and wildlife conservation in both public (government) and private organizations. In the public arena, there are jobs available through both the United States Fish & Wildlife Service and the Animal Welfare Division of the United States Department of Agriculture. Counties have animal control offices that offer many positions in which people deal with wild animals. These jobs include veterinarian, wildlife technician, and research assistant.

The World Wildlife Fund, Nature Conservancy, and the Sierra Club Legal Defense Fund are just a few private-sector wildlife organizations where you can look for opportunities. They are involved in conservation and preservation of animals and their habitats.

If you work for a protective organization, you will have little direct contact with animals. But your impact on these animals' lives can be great. The types of jobs available vary with each organization. Jobs include fundraising, public relations, marketing, and computer work. Working for a wildlife organization is ideal for animal lovers who are unable to perform the physical labor that animal care requires. Such work also has regular business hours. If you are interested in working for either the government or a private organization, contact them directly.

Each organization has its own job requirements. As with zoo careers, volunteering is a good way to gain experience that can lead to full-time employment. Salaries generally range from $12,000 to $42,000, depending on the work that you do and the agency you work for.

## Animal Shelters

Animal shelter workers enforce local animal control laws. They rescue animals and control stray or unwanted animals. They investigate complaints of animal abuse. Animal shelter workers may be called to testify in court in abuse cases.

Like zookeepers, animal shelter workers help animals directly. They are responsible for the health of the animals. They also deal with hurt or sick animals. Since the pet population is so large, animal shelter workers see animals die every day, which can be hard to take.

People who work for wildlife organizations often help raise money to sustain places such as bird sanctuaries, which provide safe places for birds to live.

Animal shelter workers are required to have a high school education. Additional education increases the types of work available. Salaries range from $12,000 to $24,000.

## Questions to Ask Yourself

There are many ways to work with animals. 1) How can you gain experience in working with animals? 2) Where can you find these opportunities?

Veterinarians have increased opportunities to do advanced or specialized work.

# Careers in Animal Care That Require a College Degree

A college education takes time, money, commitment, and a lot of hard work. The benefits of such investments for a career in animal care include:

✔ Increased and more in-depth knowledge of animals and their habits

✔ Increased career opportunities

✔ Increased salary potential

✔ Ability to attend veterinary school

✔ Opportunities to learn about other related careers

✔ Opportunity to do specialized or groundbreaking work

## Veterinary Medicine

There are many types of veterinary medicine. Small animal vets work with dogs, cats, rodents, birds, and reptiles. Large animal vets work with farm animals, racehorses, and larger zoo animals.

Like medical doctors, veterinarians can also specialize in certain areas. Some vets study just a small aspect of animal health. Others specialize in just one animal. Veterinary medicine includes such specialists as the following:

✔ Veterinary ophthalmologists, who are animal eye specialists

✔ Veterinary toxicologists, who study animal disease in a laboratory setting

✔ Equine veterinarians, who work exclusively with racehorses or on horse stud farms

✔ Veterinary dermatologists, who are animal skin specialists

✔ Veterinary nutritionists, who help select specific foods and diets for pets

✔ Veterinary acupuncturists, who treat animals by channeling energy through the placement of needles on the animals' bodies.

*The veterinary hospital where Mark works employs small animal veterinarians. Veterinary specialists also work there. Mark trained as a small animal veterinarian, but he is also a specialist. His area of expertise is emergency medicine.*

*Mark began work at the animal hospital right after graduating from veterinary school. He worked regular*

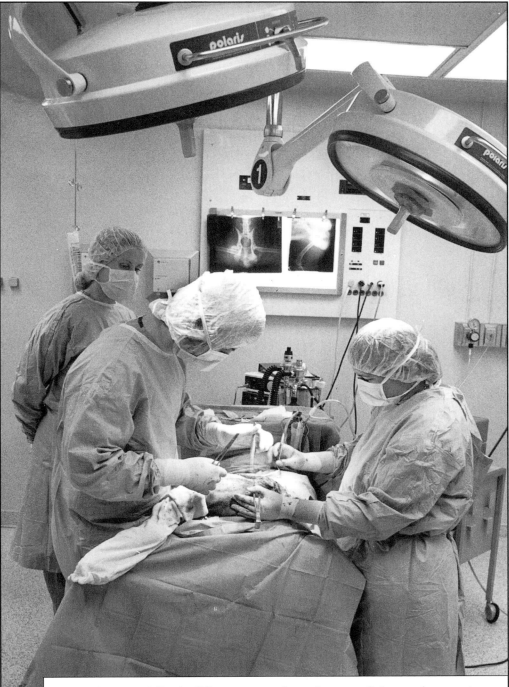

Veterinarians specialize in different areas of veterinary medicine, such as surgery.

*hours during the week for two years. Mark also worked weekends when he needed extra money.*

*The only animals admitted on weekends are those with medical emergencies. Treating emergency cases was challenging and exciting for Mark. He enjoyed it more than his regular workweek. Sometimes two hurt animals were brought in at the same time. Other times, an animal with confusing symptoms would be brought in.*

*Mark decided that he wanted to become a specialist in emergency veterinary medicine. So during his third year, Mark changed his schedule. He worked twenty hours during the week seeing regular cases, mostly cats and dogs. Mark also worked twenty hours on the weekend. That weekend experience trained him well for his specialty.*

*Mark now only works with emergency cases. In the emergency room, he treats animals that have eaten poison or have been hit by cars. He also treats animals that are suffering from disease. Together with veterinary technicians, Mark works to stabilize these sick or injured animals.*

*Ideally, an animal brought into the emergency room will be able to go home after the weekend. Mark's work is*

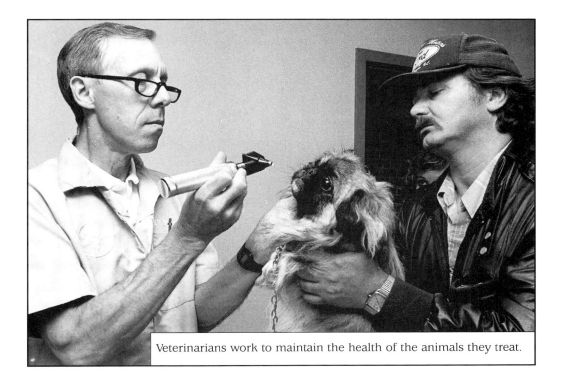
Veterinarians work to maintain the health of the animals they treat.

*always challenging and sometimes really stressful or, if the animal is in really bad shape, very sad. But at the end of the day, especially when he is able to save an animal's life or help them recover from an illness, Mark looks back and knows that there is no other work that would be more rewarding for him.*

Veterinarians do a wide variety of jobs. They examine animals, treat emergencies, and perform operations. Some work in laboratories doing research rather than working directly with animals. But they all work to improve the health of animals.

A veterinarian assumes a lot of responsibility, so the salary for this job can be quite high. Graduates start at about $20,000 to $31,000 per

**43**

year. After gaining experience, a veterinarian's salary can reach over $100,000 per year.

People who choose to become veterinarians must be able to work under stress. They often work long hours. Veterinarians also need curious minds. They must always increase their understanding of animal anatomy and disease. They need to keep up on new techniques and discoveries by reading veterinary periodicals and attending professional conferences.

Seventy percent of American veterinarians are in private practice. It is important for vets to be able to communicate well with their patients' owners. Pet owners expect a vet to explain their pet's problems clearly. To build a successful practice, vets also need to know how to run a business.

It takes a lot of dedication to become a veterinarian. First you must complete high school. Then you must earn two college degrees. The first degree is either a bachelor of arts or bachelor of science from a four-year college. The second degree is one in veterinary medicine, which can only be earned from a school of veterinary medicine. These are usually three-year programs. These schools are sometimes more difficult to get accepted into than medical schools.

Planning for a career as a veterinarian can begin in high school. You can prepare for college by taking classes in biology, chemistry, and math. Business classes such as bookkeeping also are helpful should you decide to open your own practice.

It can be difficult to get into veterinary school. Once there, the hours are long and demanding. However, for those who are accepted and those who last through the training, a career as a veterinarian is satisfying and fulfilling. Veterinarians earn more money than animal care workers without college degrees. They also have more job options available.

## Other Animal-Related Careers

There are other animal-related careers that require a college education. Wildlife biologists (people who design and conduct studies on the local wildlife) and zoo curators (those who keep track of the zoo's animals and make sure they are cared for properly) are two such careers. They both require at least an undergraduate college degree in an area such as zoology, ecology, or biology. While many animal-related professions require a graduate degree, there are satisfying careers in all aspects of animal care for those who earn a bachelor's degree.

## Questions to Ask Yourself

Animal care careers that require a college degree can be rewarding both emotionally and financially. 1) How important is earning a high salary to you? 2) Are you willing to devote the time necessary to earn a degree in an area of animal care?

# Planning and
# Preparing for a Career
# in Animal Care

Planning is an important part of any career. Planning helps you focus on a career that best fits your interests and skills and to be prepared to take advantage of opportunities when they arise. Preparation follows careful planning. Career preparation involves finding the right type of training or education and talking with people who work in the career you have chosen to explore.

## Planning a Career

Planning and choosing a career is an important and often difficult process. You need to be honest with yourself about your skills and interests. When your job goals are clearly defined, you will be able to find a career that will be satisfying.

Now that you've narrowed your career choice down to a career in animal care, how do you choose which type of animal care? The questions in chapter 1 can help you narrow down the

You might try out a career in animal care by starting a dog-walking business.

choices. Keep those answers in mind while you read the following planning survey, which will help you pinpoint the best animal care career for you.

## Planning Survey

Planning a career requires a close match between interests, skills, and available jobs. The following outline is a good first step in planning a career in animal care.

### Careers working directly with animals and being responsible for their care:

Animal groomer

Animal or kennel attendant

Animal trainer

Pet sitter

Pet walker

Veterinarian

Veterinary assistant

Veterinary technician

Zoo exhibit curator (zoo keeper)

## Careers that require working outside:

Animal trainer

Park ranger

Pet walker

Zoo keeper

## Careers that require working inside:

Animal groomer

Animal or kennel attendant

Animal shelter worker

Laboratory animal caretaker

Pet sitter

Pet store employee

Pet store owner

Veterinarian

Veterinary assistant

Veterinary technician

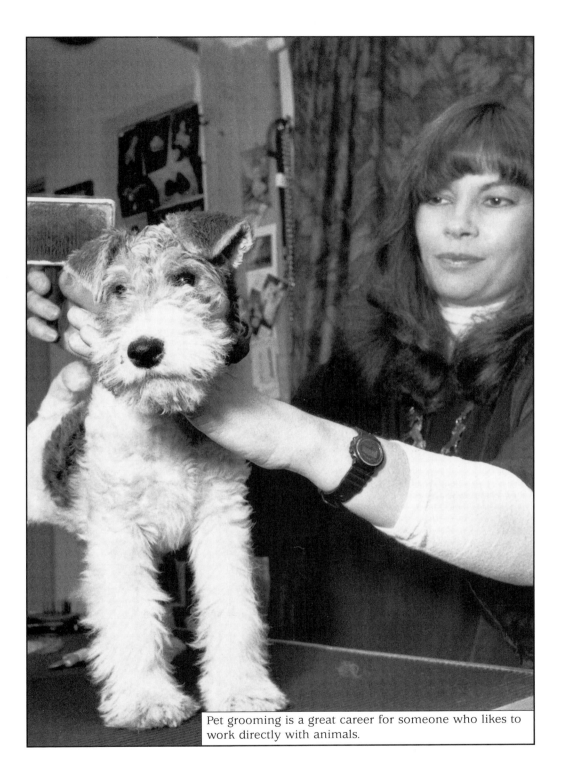

Pet grooming is a great career for someone who likes to work directly with animals.

## Careers that require the ability to work with other people:

Animal groomer

Animal or kennel attendant

Animal rights activist

Park ranger

Pet store employee

Pet store owner

Veterinarian

Veterinary assistant

## Careers that require less contact with people:

Animal artist

Laboratory animal caretaker

Pet sitter

Pet walker

## Careers that require further education:

Conservationist

Resource coordinator

Veterinarian

Wildlife biologist

Zoo curator

## Unusual Careers

Sometimes people with unusual skills or experiences create their own careers or businesses. These people are called entrepreneurs. There are many possibilities in animal care for entrepreneurs. A few examples are:

Animal illustrator

Animal masseuse

Animal transporter or animal taxi driver

Endangered-animal breeder

Pet photographer

Pet therapist

Once you decide which areas interest you, follow up on your hard work and soul-searching by talking to people in those careers. They can tell you how they became interested in the career, what they like and don't like about it, and how to get more information about it.

*During his senior year of high school, Jack began to worry. Most of his friends had career plans. They knew what they wanted to do after high school. But Jack had no idea what he wanted to do. How could he decide? He didn't have a plan.*

*Jack had never had a job or volunteered his time anywhere. He spent most*

Veterinarians may have to work with guide dogs, who are essential to the safety of their vision-impaired owners.

*of his free time working on his hobby. He was an amateur woodworker.*

*Most of Jack's projects had been gifts for friends or relatives. He had never considered using his skills as a career. But when he delivered a doghouse to his aunt, she gave him an idea.*

*"This doghouse is beautiful!" exclaimed Jack's aunt. "Are they hard to make? You could easily sell them."*

*Jack's aunt loved pets. She bought all kinds of things for her dogs. She knew what was available at pet stores. She had never seen anything quite like Jack's doghouse at any store.*

*Jack thought about the idea of using his woodworking skills for a career. Making specialty doghouses for pet lovers would be fun. Jack started to plan a business to manufacture doghouses. He made a list of his skills. He also listed skills needed to achieve his goal. Once his lists were complete, Jack was excited.*

*Building up a new business would take time and patience. But with his plan, Jack felt confident. He finally knew where he was going.*

## Preparing for an Animal Care Career

Before you choose a career in an animal care field, you should learn as much about it as possible. If you know someone who has the job you think you'd like, do an informational interview. Sit down with them and ask them everything you'd like to know about their career. You're not asking them for a job, just for information.

You can also volunteer or do an internship with an organization. If you want to work with abandoned animals, call the local shelter to see if you can volunteer. Wildlife and animal rights organizations almost always need volunteers and some offer internships, which give you a chance to work inside the organization. Both of these options offer the opportunity to get a sense of what the job is really like.

Working during summer vacations is also a great way to experience a career firsthand. Many animal care businesses, such as grooming salons and pet stores, hire temporary employees during the summer months.

It's always good to research a career beforehand as well. Public libraries have many books available, as well as a wide selection of interest-specific magazines like *Dog World* and *Cat Fancy*. Surfing the Internet can also provide you with a lot of information and contacts. By doing research you can also learn about other related careers you might not have thought about.

You can also write to professional organizations and ask them to send you information about what they do and job opportunities that they may have available. They also may be able to refer you to local organizations and schools for information and training. It might seem like a lot of work, but if it helps you decide on a job that's right for you, then it's worth it.

## Questions to Ask Yourself

Choosing a particular career within animal care may be difficult. 1) Have you been honest with yourself about your skills, interests, likes, and dislikes? 2) How can you find more information about the career you are interested in?

# 5

# Getting Started in Animal Care

Now that you know which direction you want to take, you need to know how to reach your goal of getting a job in the field. One way is through volunteering the way Elaine, the assistant zookeeper, did. Another is to apply for a job directly. You can find job listings in industry magazines, the classified section of local news-papers, and by inquiring at local vendors such as pet stores, veterinarian offices, groomers, and zoos. You might also try contacting the organizations listed at the back of this book for more tips on job-hunting in a particular field.

Once you've located a few job openings, you must apply for those jobs. To do this you must have the required education, some skills in the area, and a knockout résumé.

## Your Résumé

A résumé, French for "summary," is a written summary of your education, work history, training, and skills. A résumé is usually requested when you apply for a job. It is your chance to make a good first impression.

Your résumé shows you have planned for a career. If you don't have work experience, highlight your volunteer experience. Any related hobby or school club can also be listed.

Review your résumé several times to make sure you have included the information you think is important and have recorded it accurately. The final version of your résumé should be mistake-free and neatly typed on good paper.

Once you've turned in your résumé and application, you may be called for an interview, the final step in getting a job. There are many books on proper interviewing techniques. You can study up on some of them by checking out those books at the library.

Getting a job is a lot of work. But when you consider that you spend one-third of your life working, it's worth the effort it takes to find a career that you love.

## Questions to Ask Yourself

There are several methods for finding a job. 1) Where can you find the classifieds in your local paper? 2) What sort of animal care facilities are in your community? 3) How can you contact them?

# Glossary

**animal rights activists**   People who work to save animals who need protection.

**commission**   Income earned based on the amount of work done or products sold.

**conservation**   A careful preservation and protection of something..

**curator**   Person in charge of zoo exhibits.

**emergency**   Time of sudden need.

**endangered species**   Animal breeds that are being destroyed in the wild.

**entrepreneurs**   People who create their own careers or businesses.

**euthanasia**   Destroying or killing unwanted or dying animals.

**grooming**   Caring for the physical appearance of an animal.

**internship**   Training or working as an intern, someone who is doing practical supervised training.

**masseuse**   Someone who gives massages professionally.

**rapport**   Relationship; communication.

**résumé**    Summary of education, skills, and experience.

**salary**    Specified amount of money earned per year.

**surgery**  Treating diseases or medical problems by operating on the patient.

**technician**   Person who helps the professional in a given field.

**veterinarian**   Medical doctor for animals.

**volunteer**   To work for free in order to learn a job or help an organization.

WPW

# For More Information

## In the United States

American Veterinary Medical Association
1931 North Meacham Road, Suite 100
Schaumburg, IL 60173
(800) 248-2862
Web site: http://www.avma.org

American Zoo and Aquarium Association
8403 Colesville Road, Suite 710
Silver Spring, MD 20910-3314
(301) 562-0777
Web site: http://www.aza.org

American Society for the Prevention of Cruelty to
    Animals (ASPCA)
Animal Rescue
424 East 92nd Street
New York, NY 10128
(212) 876-7700
Web site: http://www.aspca.org

National Association of Professional Pet Sitters
1030 15th Street NW, Suite 870

Washington, DC 20005
(202) 393-3317
Web site: http://www.petsitters.org

World Wildlife Fund & The Conservation Foundation, Inc.
1250 24th Street NW
Washington, DC 20037-1175
(202) 293-4800
Web site: http://www.panda.org

## In Canada

Humane Society of Canada
347 Bay Street, Suite 806
Toronto, ON M5H 2R7
(800) 641-KIND (5463)
Web site: http://www.humanesociety.com

Fauna Foundation
P.O. Box 33
Chambly, PQ J3L 4B1
(450) 658-1844
Web site: http://www.faunafoundation.org

Zoological Society of Manitoba
P.O. Box 20159
Charleswood Post Office
Winnepeg, MB R3R 3R2
(204) 982-0660
Web site: http://www.zoosociety.com

## Web Sites

American Association of Zoo Keepers
http://www.aazk.org

Fancy Publications (publisher of various animal magazines)
http://www.animalnetwork.com

WɅW

# For Further Reading

Camenson, Blythe. *Opportunities in Zoo Careers.* Lincolnwood, IL: NTC Contemporary Publishing Company, 1997.

Hogan, Linda, Deena Metzger, and Brenda Peterson. *Intimate Nature: The Bond between Women and Animals.* New York: Fawcett Book Group, 1999.

Lee, Mary Price, and Richard S. Lee. *Opportunities in Animal and Pet Care Careers.* Lincolnwood, IL: NTC Contemporary Publishing Company, 1994.

Miller, Louise. *Animals.* Lincolnwood, IL: VGM Career Horizons, 1995.

———. *Careers for Animals Lovers and Other Zoological Types.* Lincolnwood, IL: NTC Contemporary Publishing Company, 1991.

Paige, David. *A Day in the Life of a Marine Biologist.* Mahwah, NJ: Troll Communication L.L.C. 1997.

Shorto, Russell. *Careers for Animal Lovers.* Brookfield, CT: Millbrook Press, Inc., 1992.

# Index

## About the Author

Jane Hurwitz earned an MA in economics from the University of Kansas. She is the co-author of *Sally Ride, Shooting for the Stars,* and *Staying Healthy,* as well as the author of *Coping in a Blended Family* and *High Performance Through Effective Budgeting.* She has always loved animals.

## Photo Credits

Cover © Shelly Gazin/Corbis; p. 2 © Evan Johnson/Impact Visuals; p. 7 © Jim West/Impact Visuals; p. 14 © Kirk Condyles/Impact Visuals; p. 18 © Soble/Klonsky/Image Bank; p. 20 © Ken Levinson/International Stock; p. 22 © David Maung/Impact Visuals; p. 25 by Adriana Skura; p. 28 © Vince Dewitt/Impact Visuals; p. 30 © Superstock; p. 33 © Jeffry Scott/Impact Visuals; pp. 34, 49 © F. M. Kearney/Impact Visuals; p. 36 © Michael Kaufman/Impact Visuals; pp. 38, 43, 52 © Martha Tabor/Impact Visuals; p. 41 © Tom Benton/Impact Visuals; p. 47 © Tom McKitterick/Impact Visuals.